AF365228

MASTER ALEXANDER SANER
Spitalstrasse 45,
4226 Breitenbach, Switzerland
a.saner@bluewin.ch

In copertina - on cover: Cut 66, 90x80x33 cm, steel

The creativity of Alexander Saner finds its way into the modelling of elegant objects, evident narrators of themselves, also talented witnesses and mastery of the technique. The source of inspiration is the reality, both as nature and as physical knowledge. With Saner everything becomes subject to artistic, profound and meticulous attention, cared for in every detail to better make the subject narrated.

La creatività di Alexander Saner trova il suo sfogo nella modellazione di oggetti eleganti, narratori palesi di se stessi, testimoni di talento e padronanza della tecnica. Fonte d'ispirazione è il reale, inteso sia come natura anche come le conoscenze fisiche. Con Saner tutto diviene oggetto di attenzione artistica, profonda e meticolosa, curata in ogni dettaglio per meglio rendere il soggetto narrato.

Dino Marasà

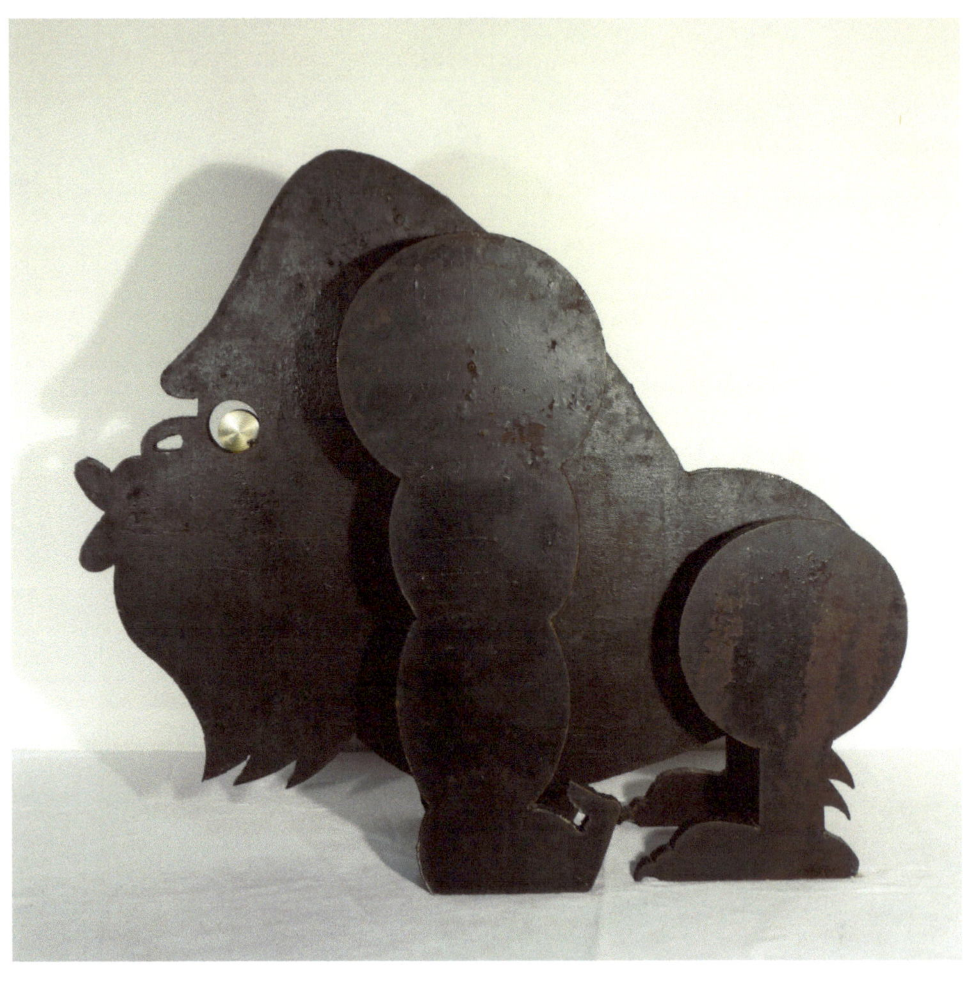

IRONic animal, Gorilla, 88x77x27 cm, iron, steel

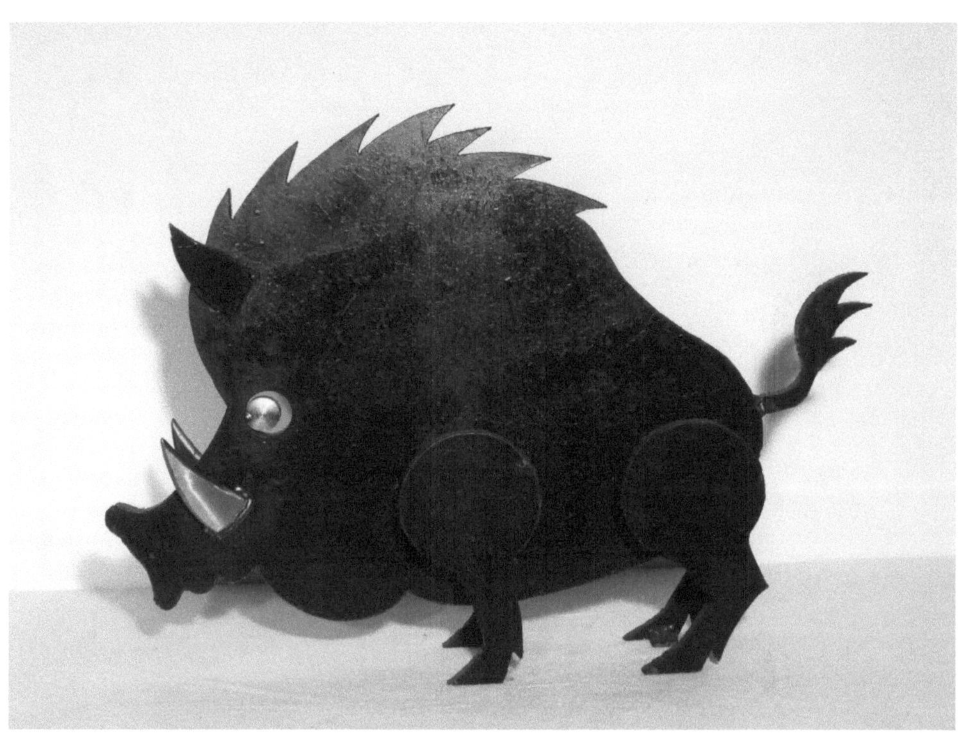

IRONic animal, Wild boar, 82x66x15 cm, iron, steel

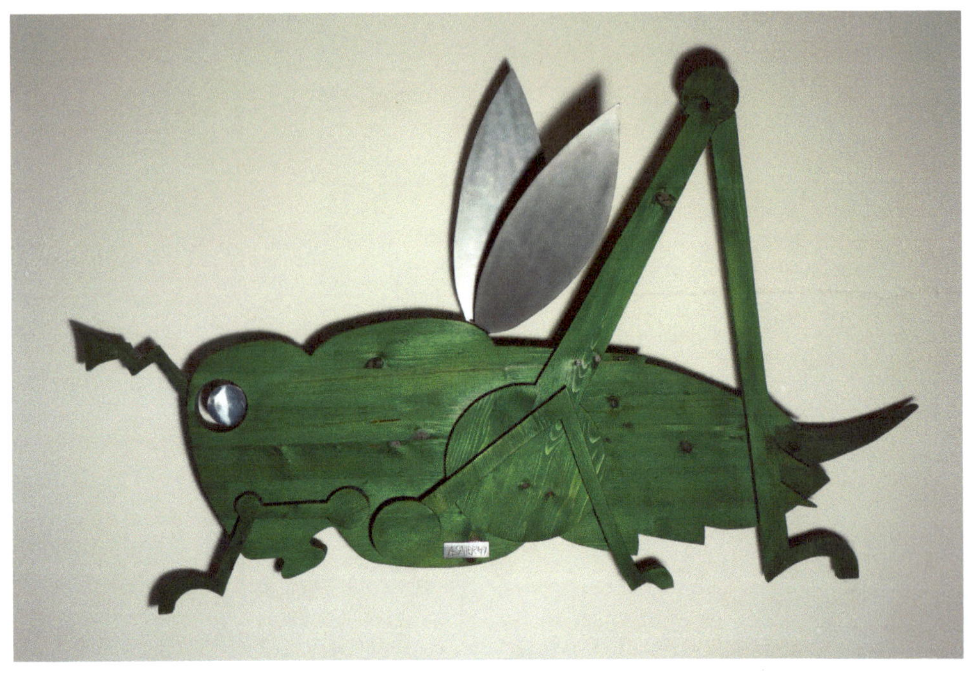

IRONic animal, Grasshopper, 104x64x19 cm, wood, aluminium

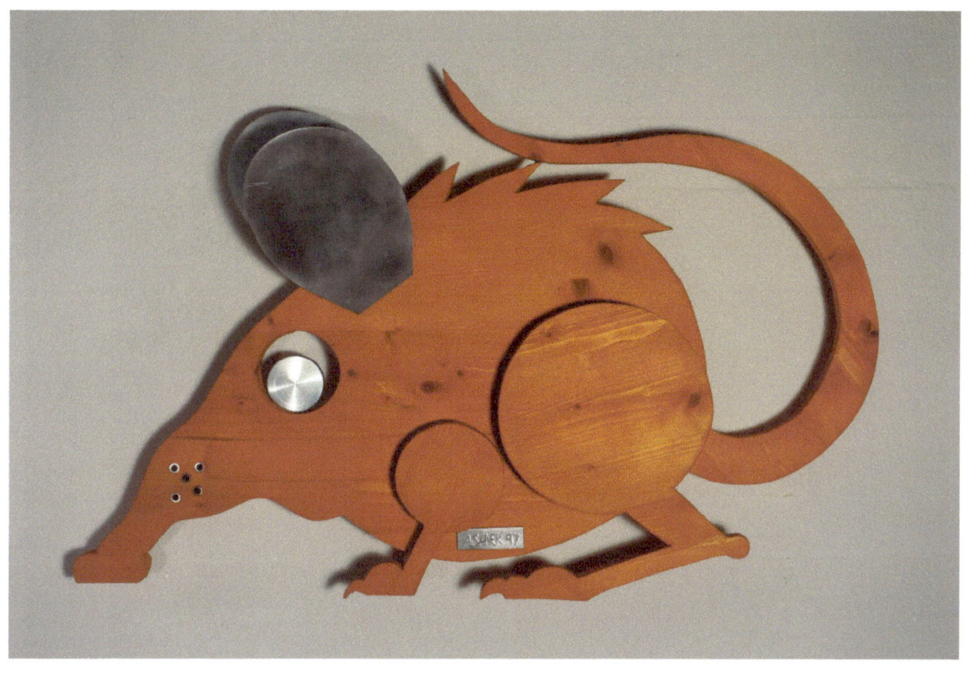

IRONic animal, North African elephant shrew, 75x50x17 cm, wood, aluminium

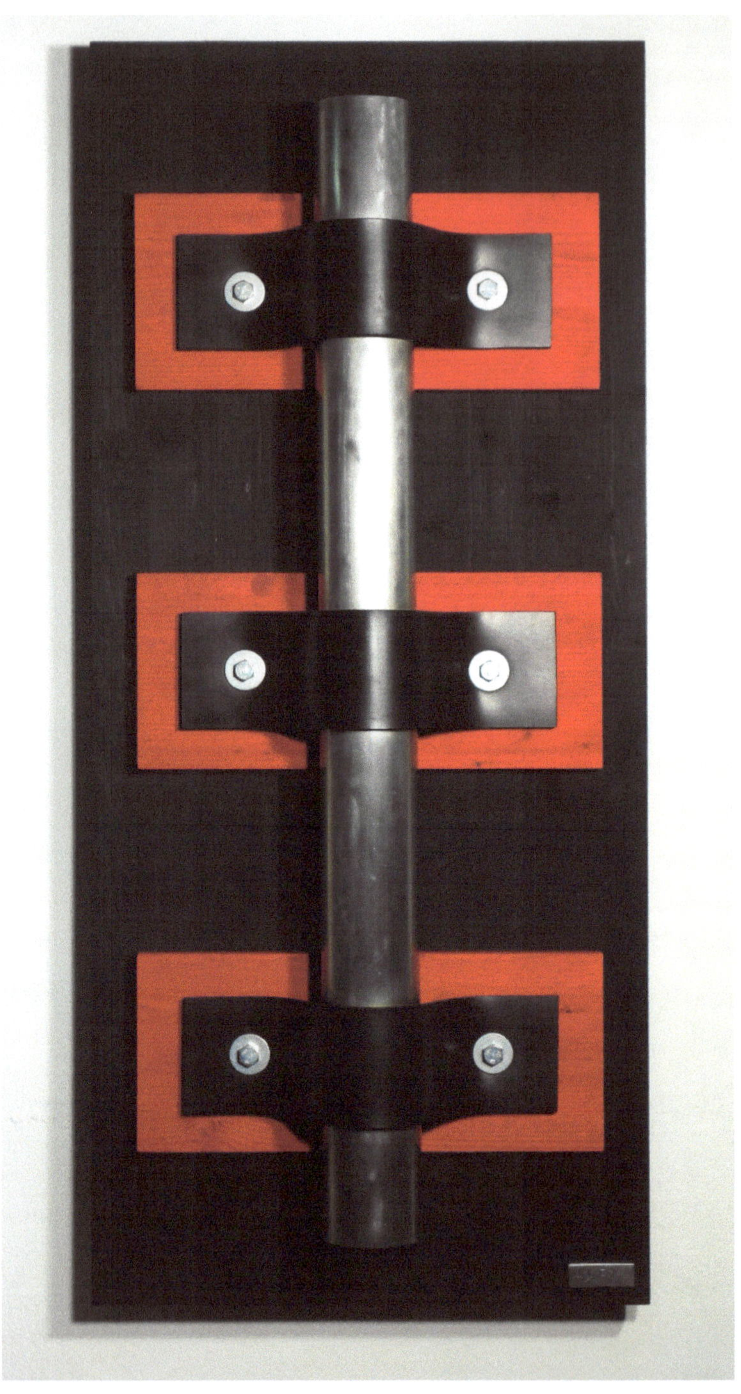

No-thing-object No.33, 49x110x20 cm, wood, steel, rubber

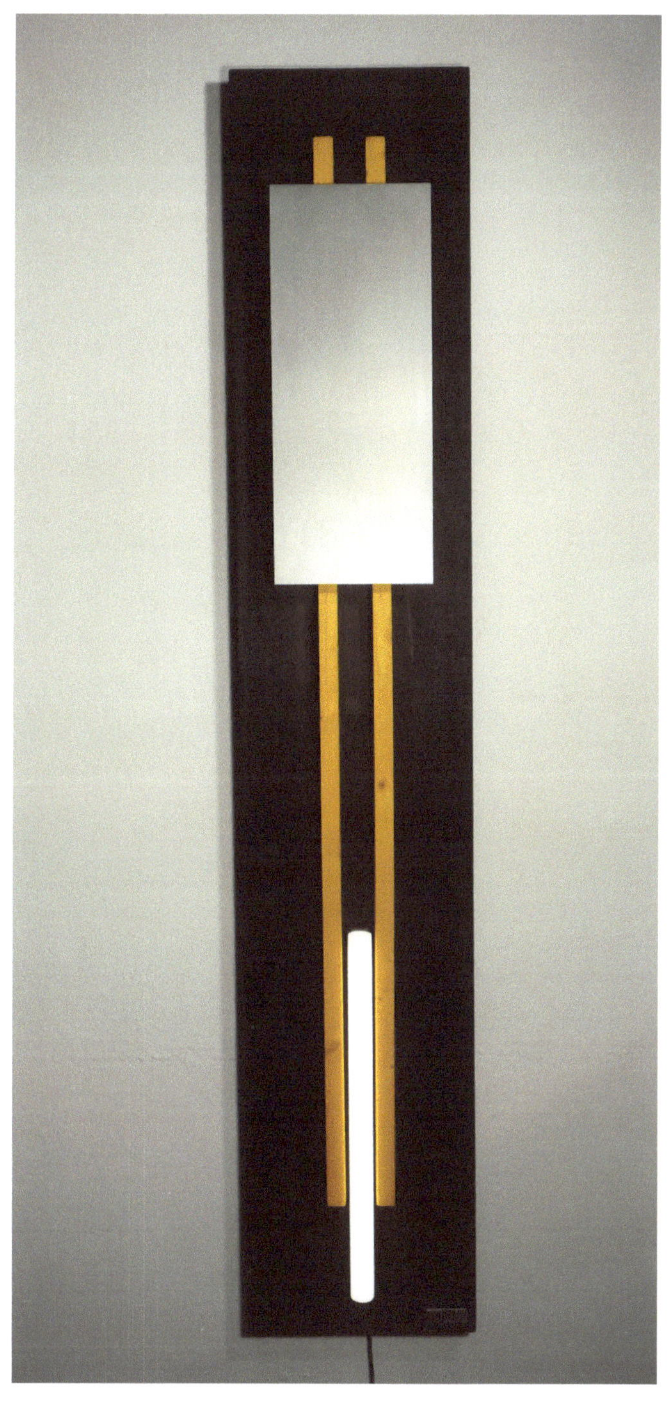

No-thing-object No.69, 31x170x12 cm, wood, metal, glass

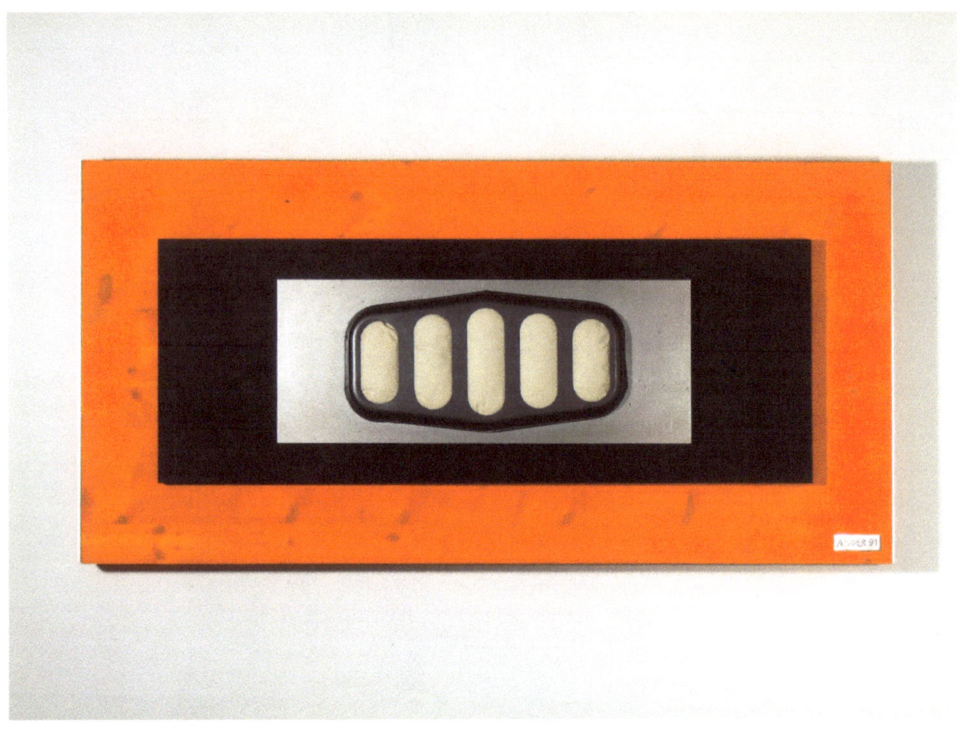

No-thing-object No.67, 100x50x14 cm, wood, metal, textile

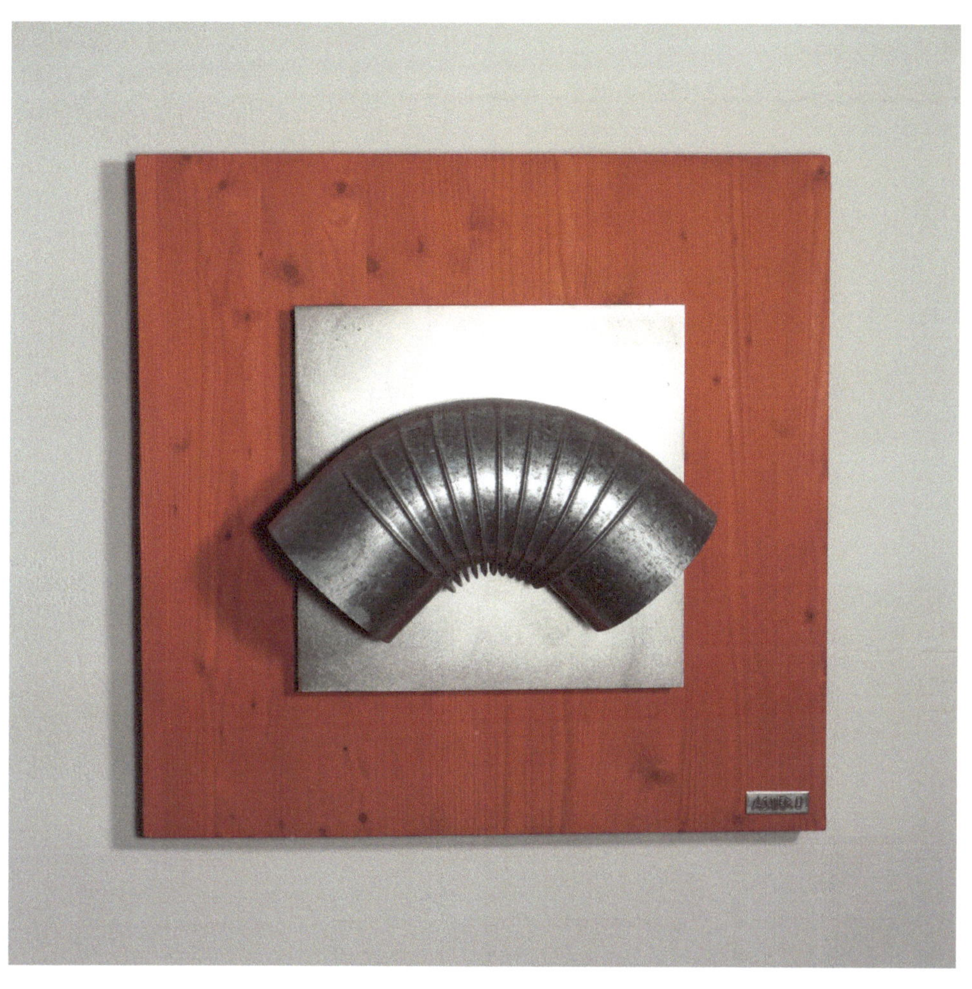

No-thing-object No.70, 60x60x25cm, wood, metal

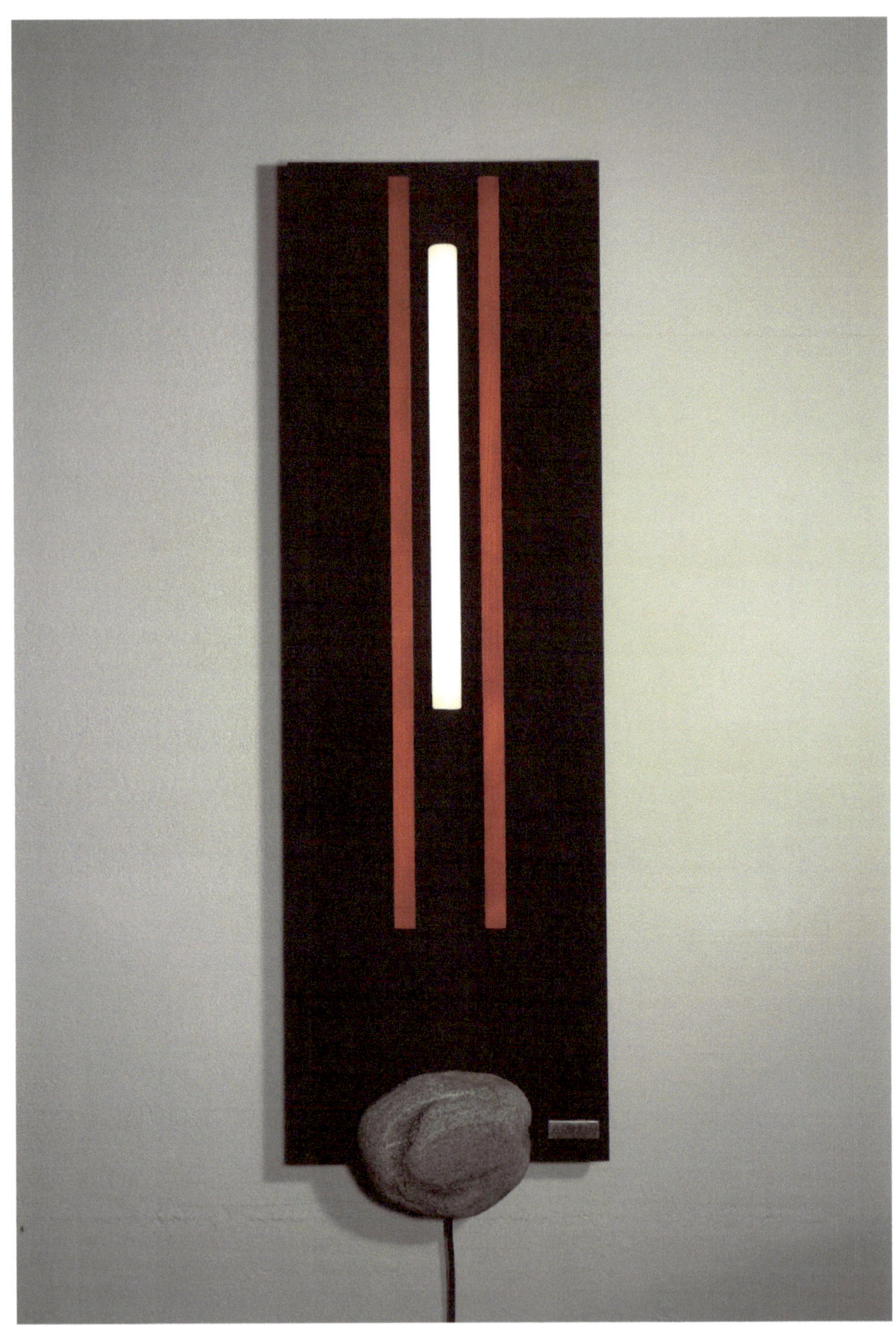

No-thing-object No.31, 34x114x14 cm, wood, stone, glass

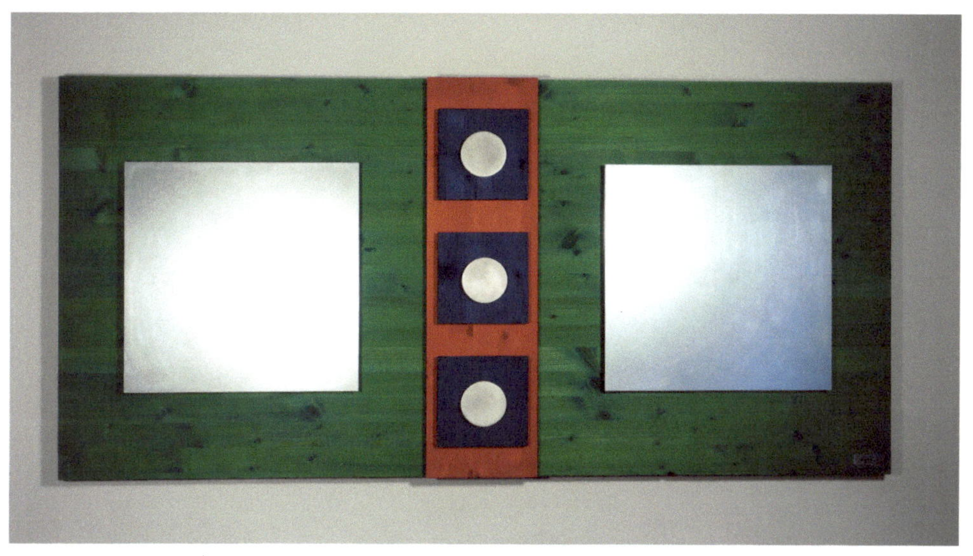

No-thing-object No.88, 150x72x13 cm, wood, metal

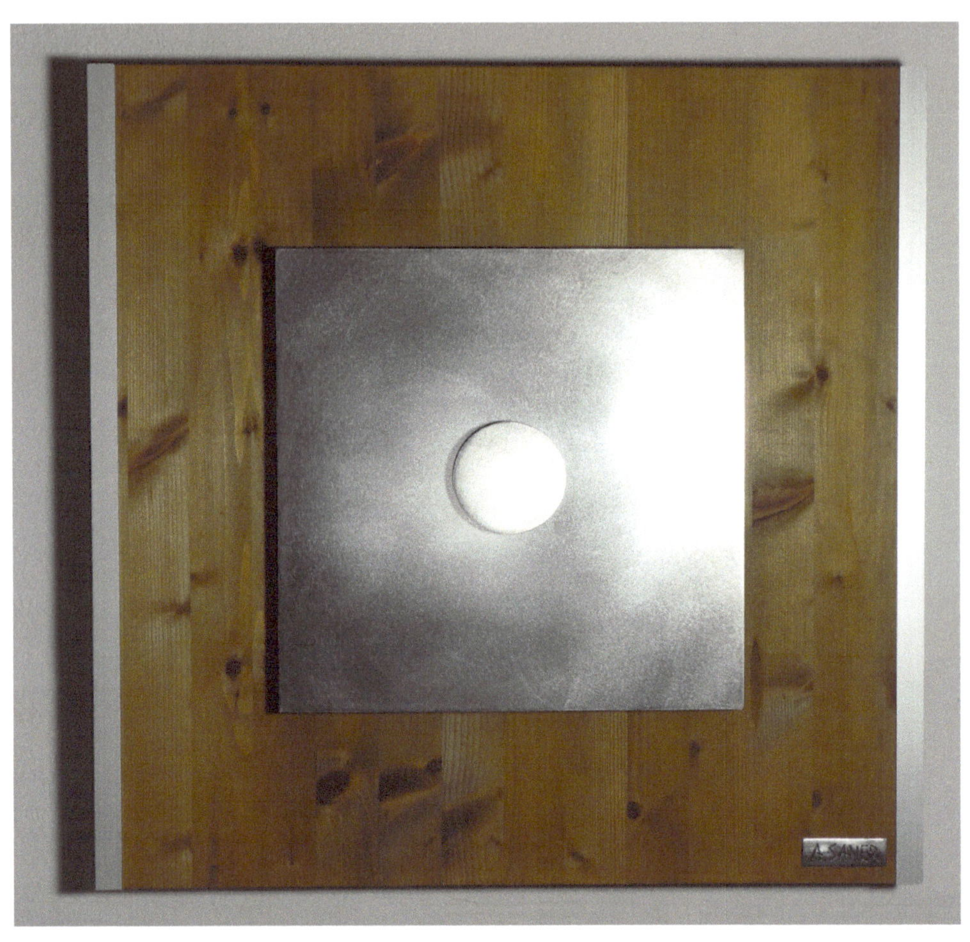

No-thing-object No.63, 60x60x14 cm, wood, metal

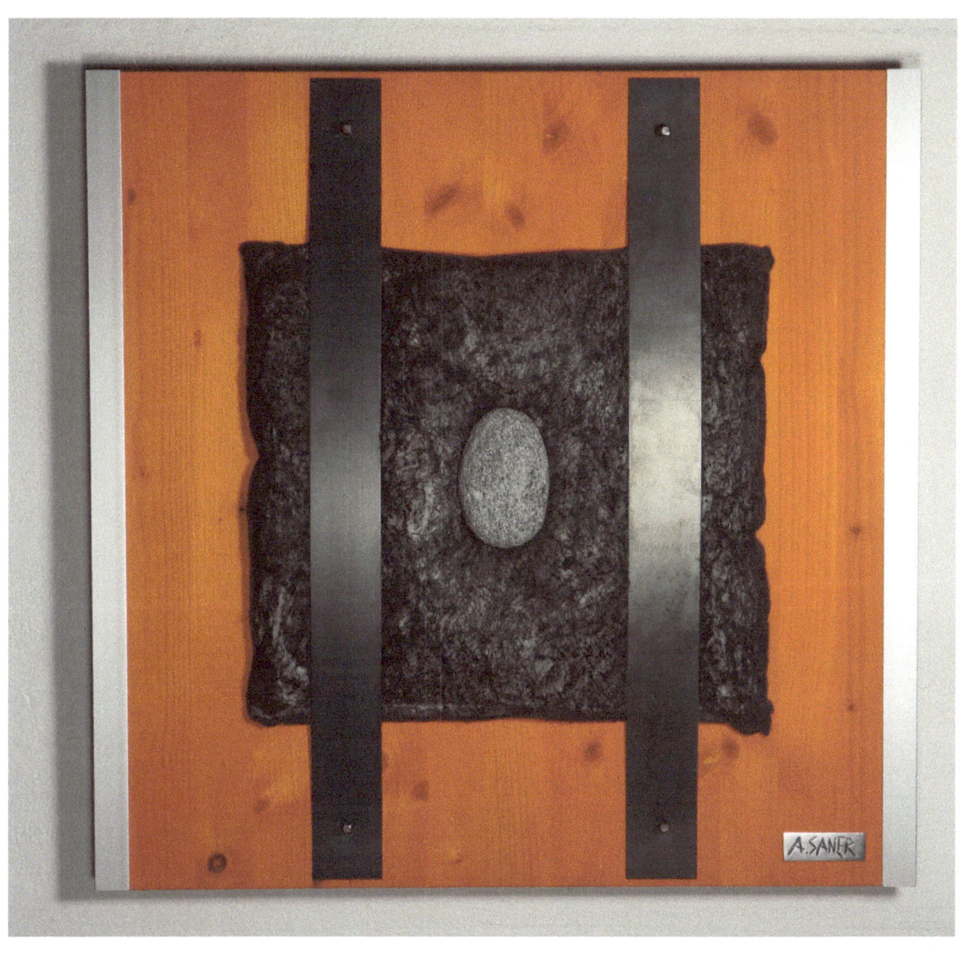

No-thing-object No.50, 60x60x11 cm, wood, stone, metal, textile

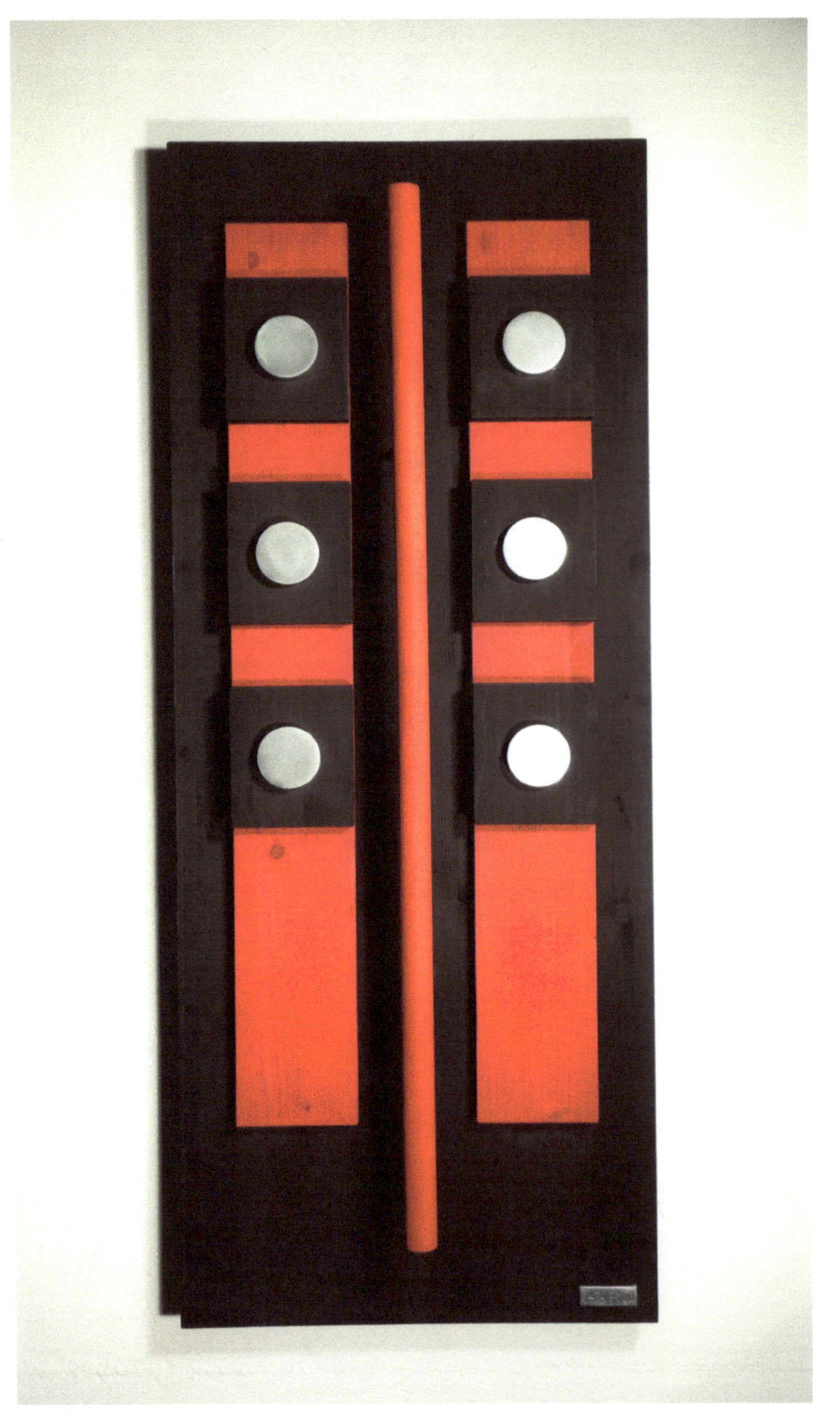

No-thing-object No.43, 48x120x18 cm, wood, aluminium

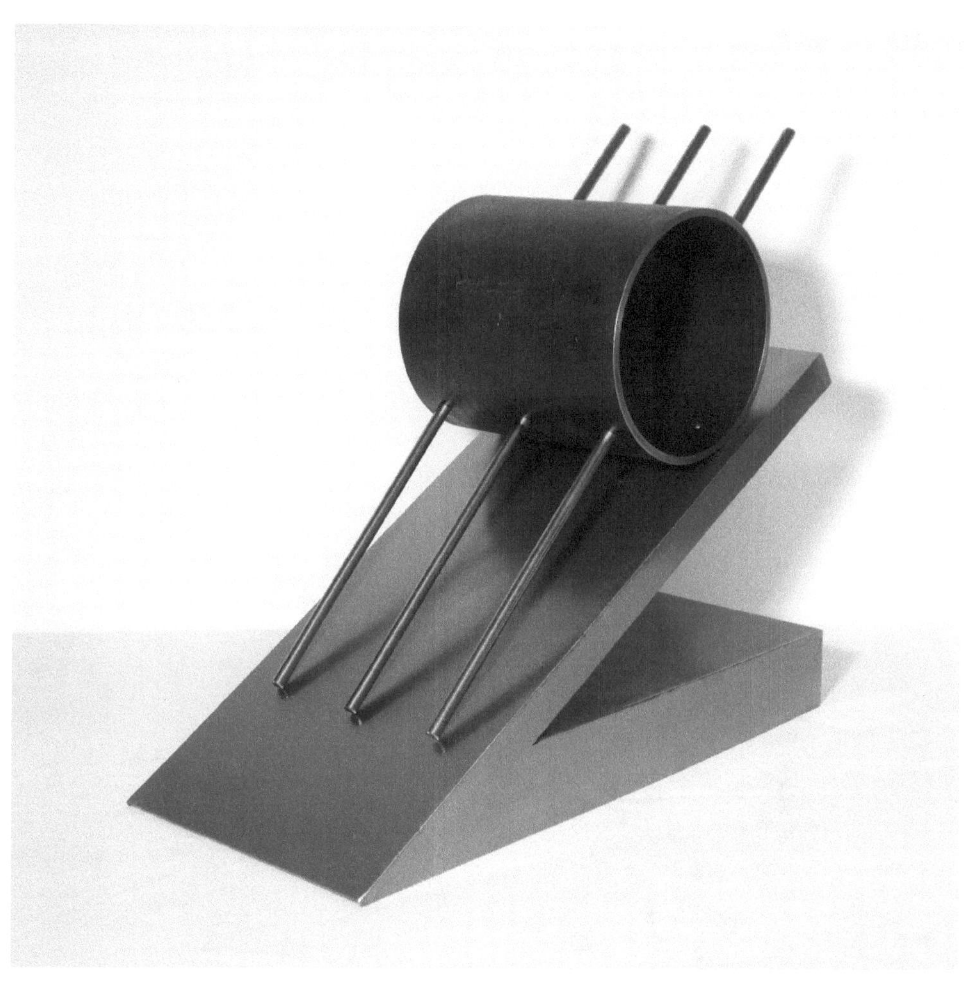

Static 3, 26x57x52 cm, steel

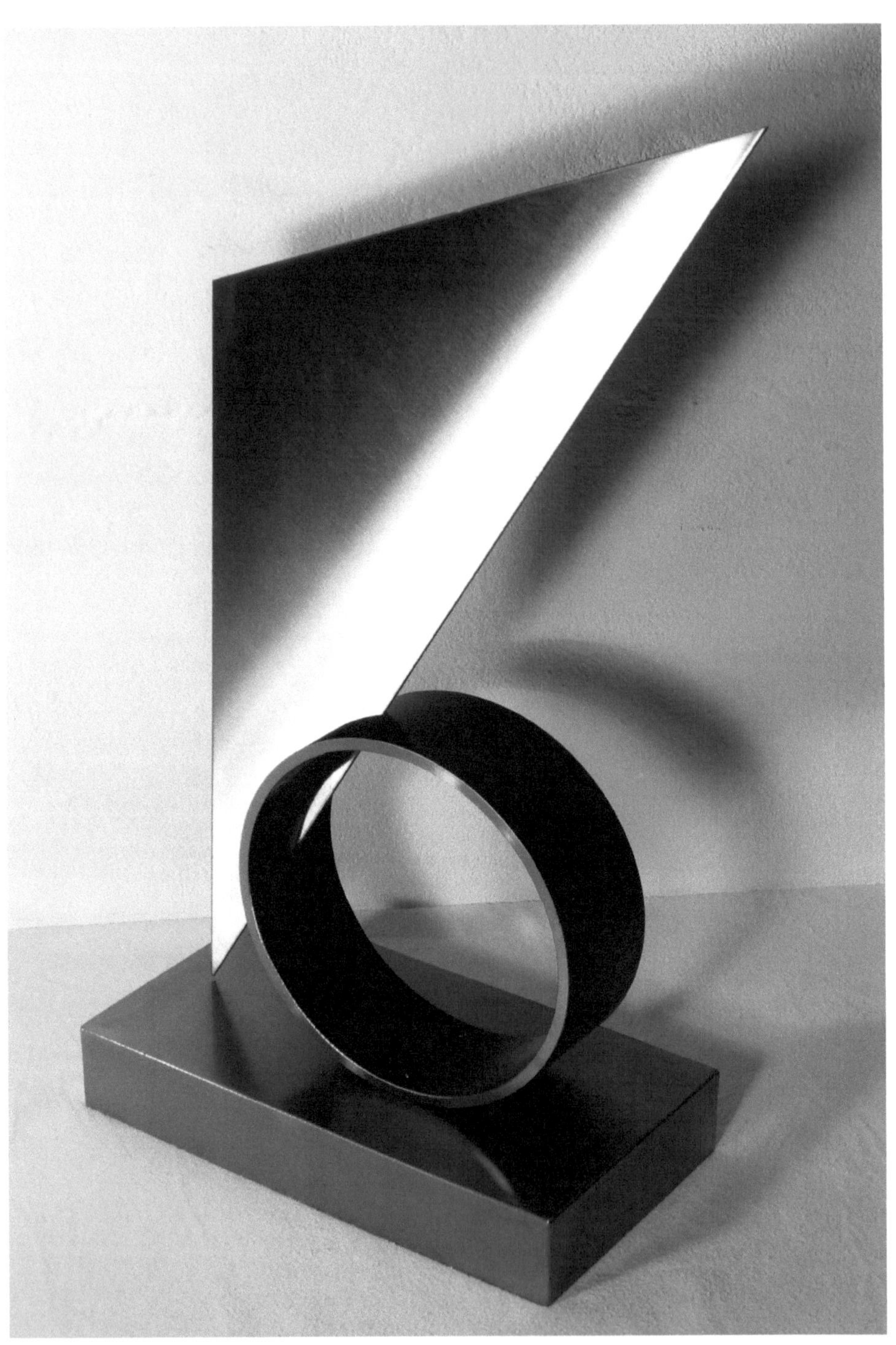

Cut 11, 16x30x58 cm, steel

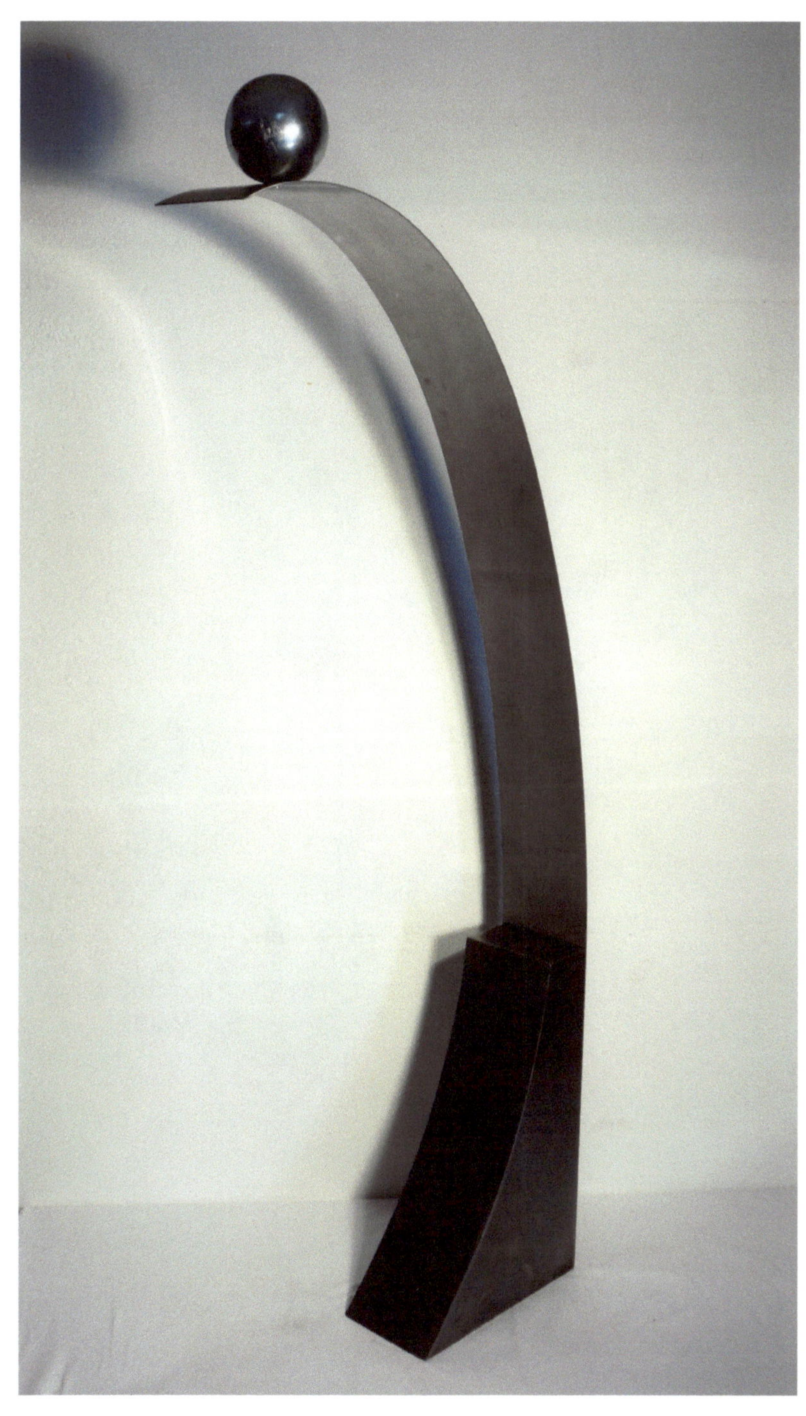

Dynamic-static 22, 16x33x170 cm, steel

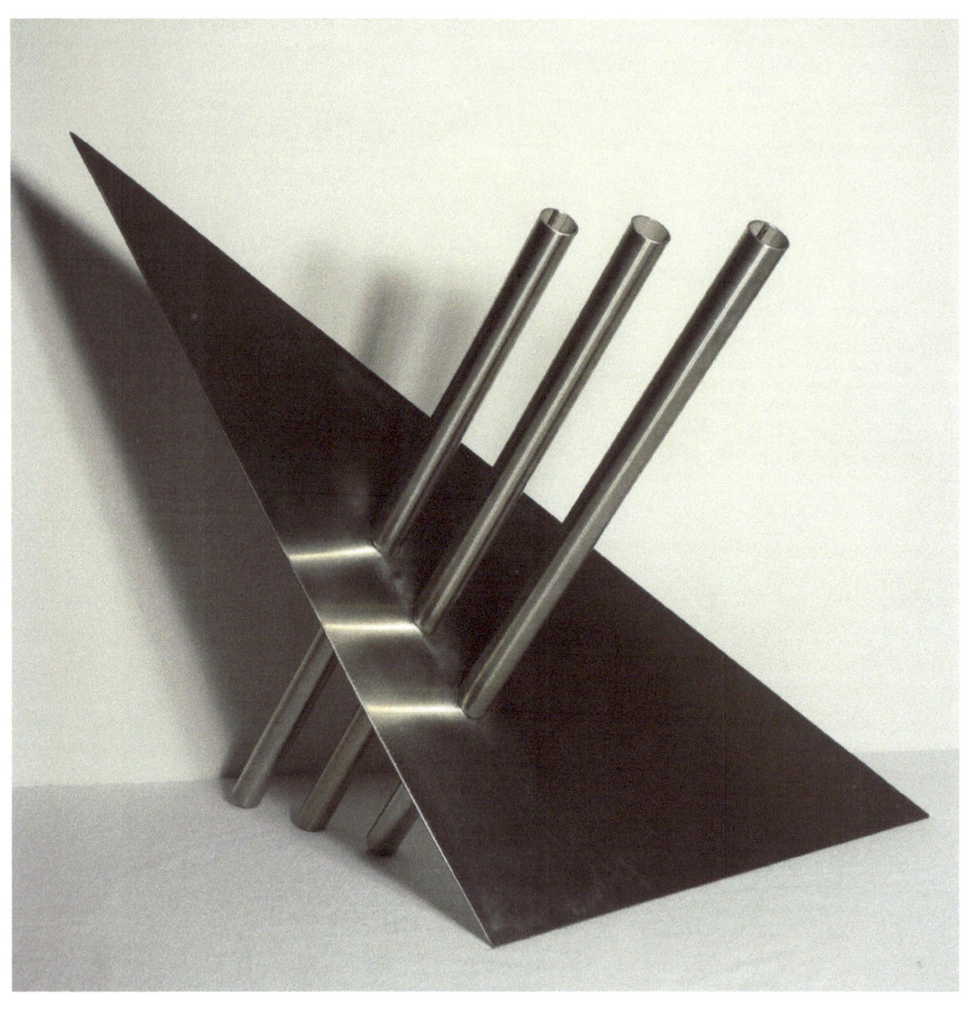

Into space, 77x71x70 cm, steel

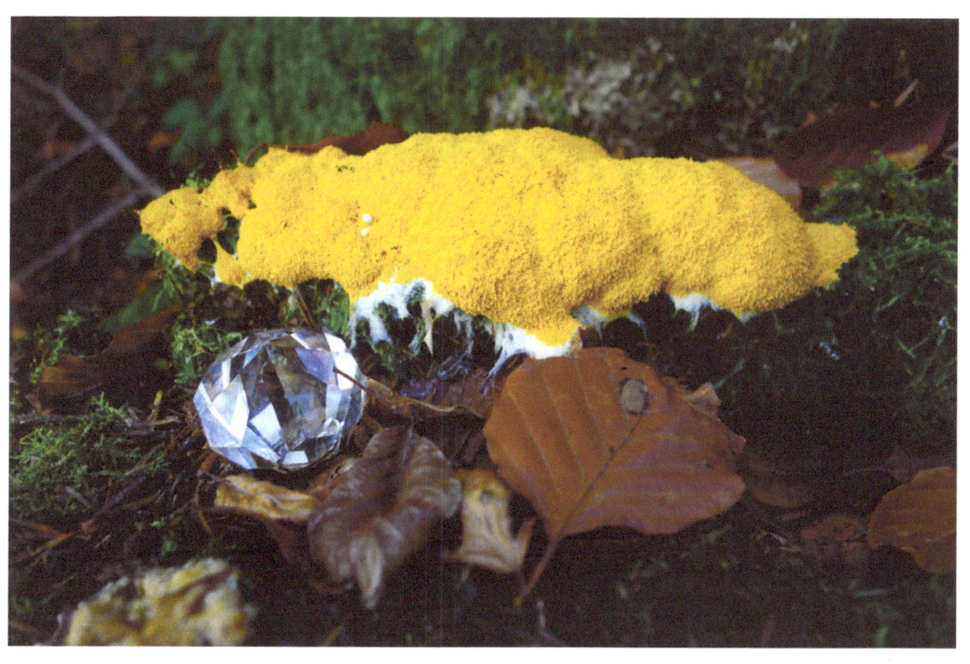

Silence 1, photography, 105x70 cm, Print Fuji Crystal ultra HD

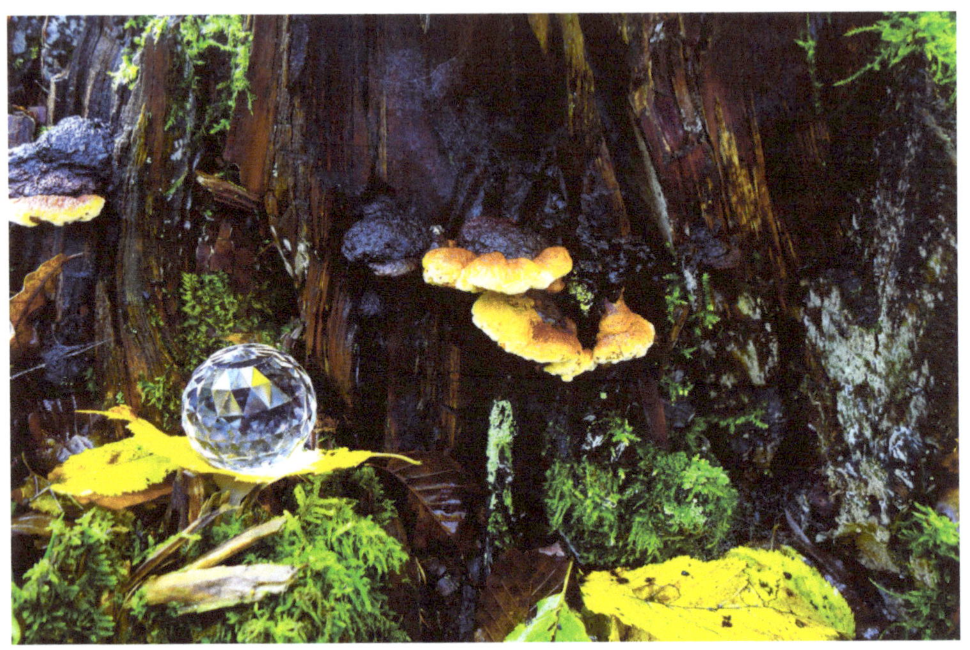

Silence 12, photography, 105x70 cm, Print Fuji Crystal ultra HD

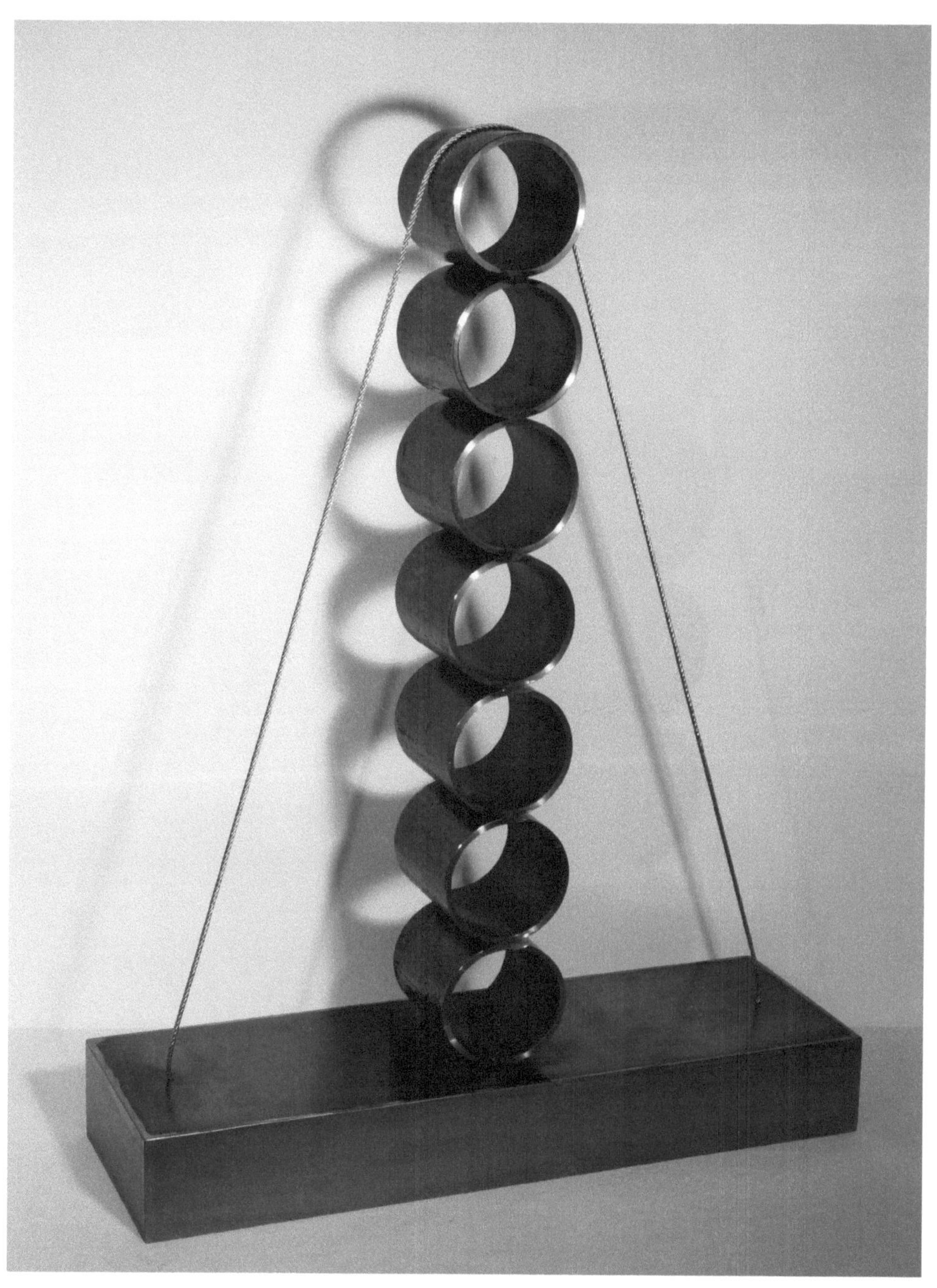

Tension 1, 30x92x125 cm, steel

21

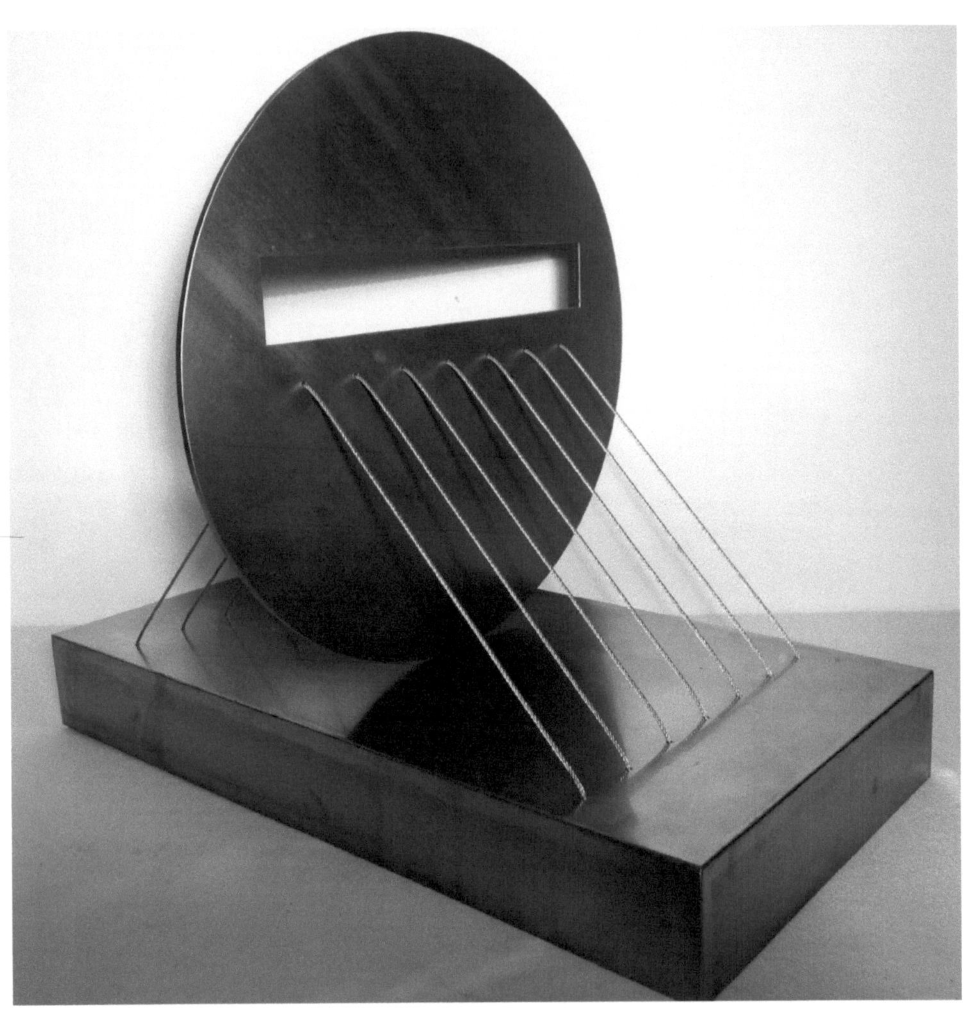

Tension 7, 36x70x60 cm, steel

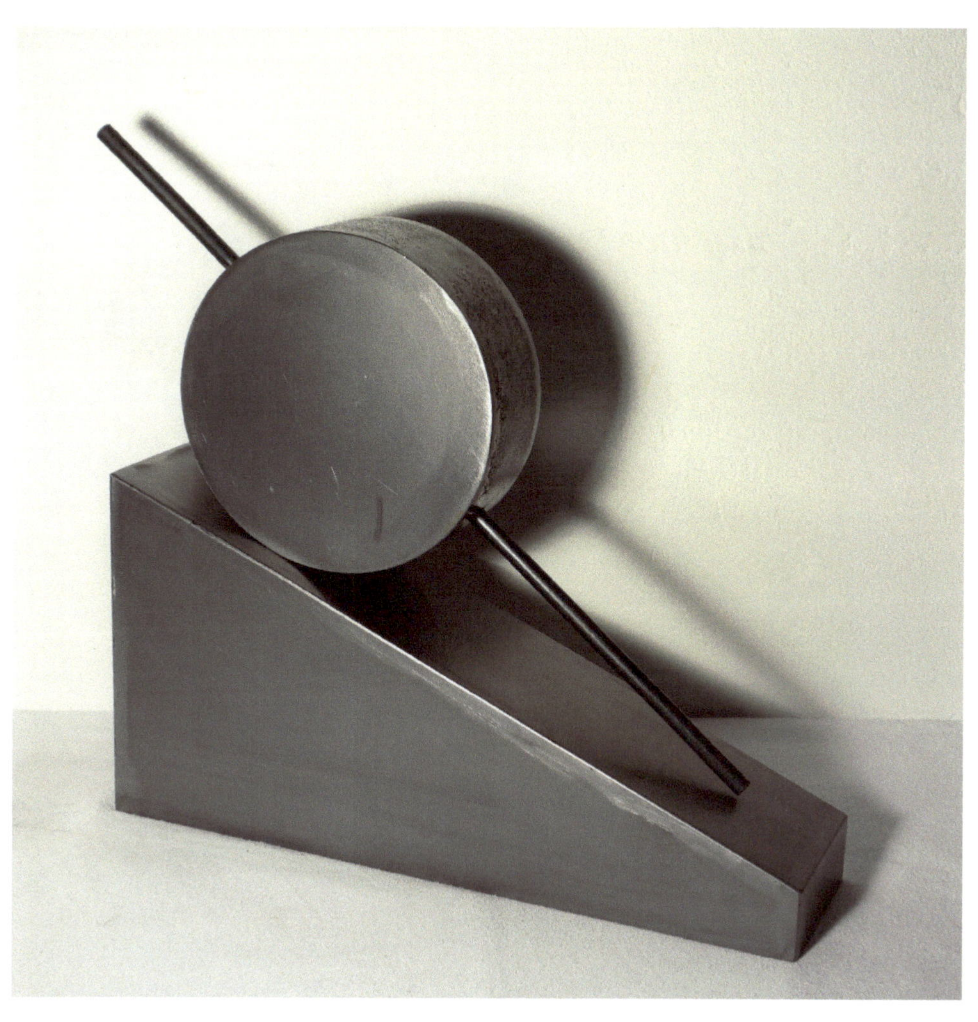

Static 1, 12x27x41 cm, steel

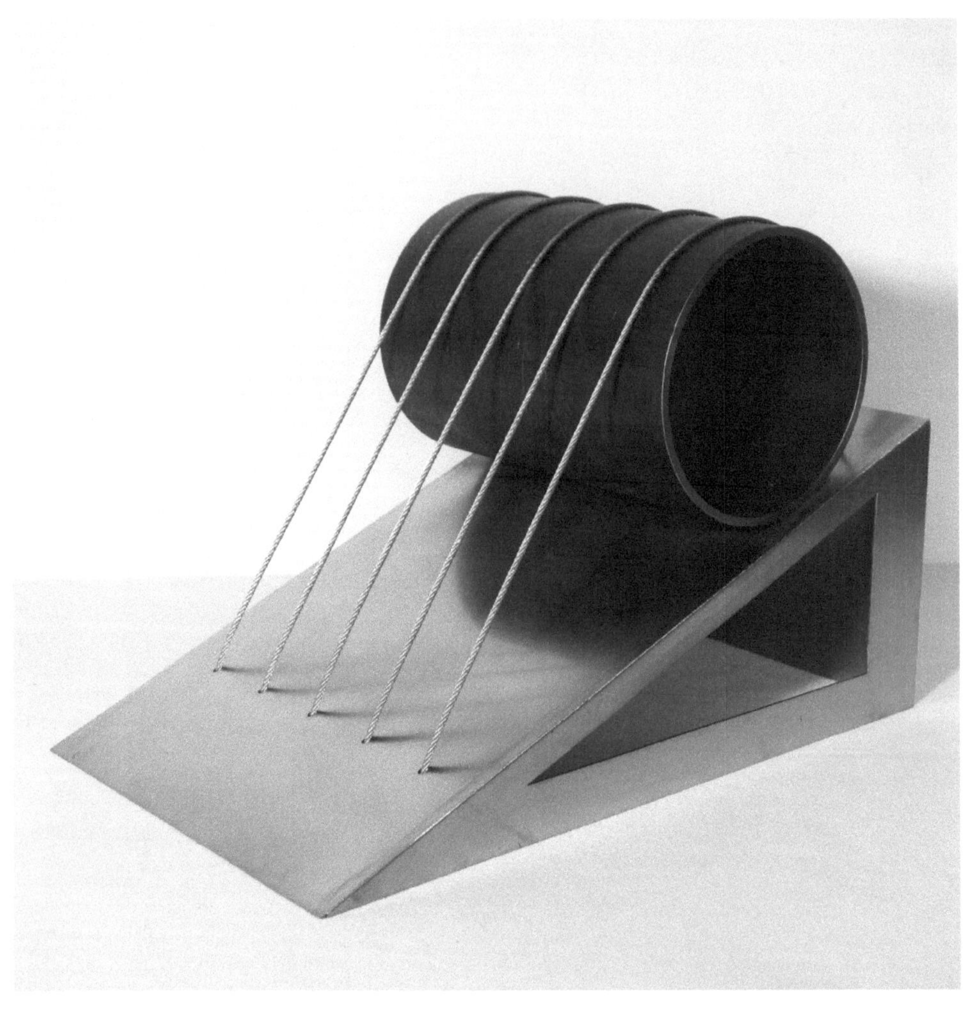

Tension 5, 33x54x48 cm, steel

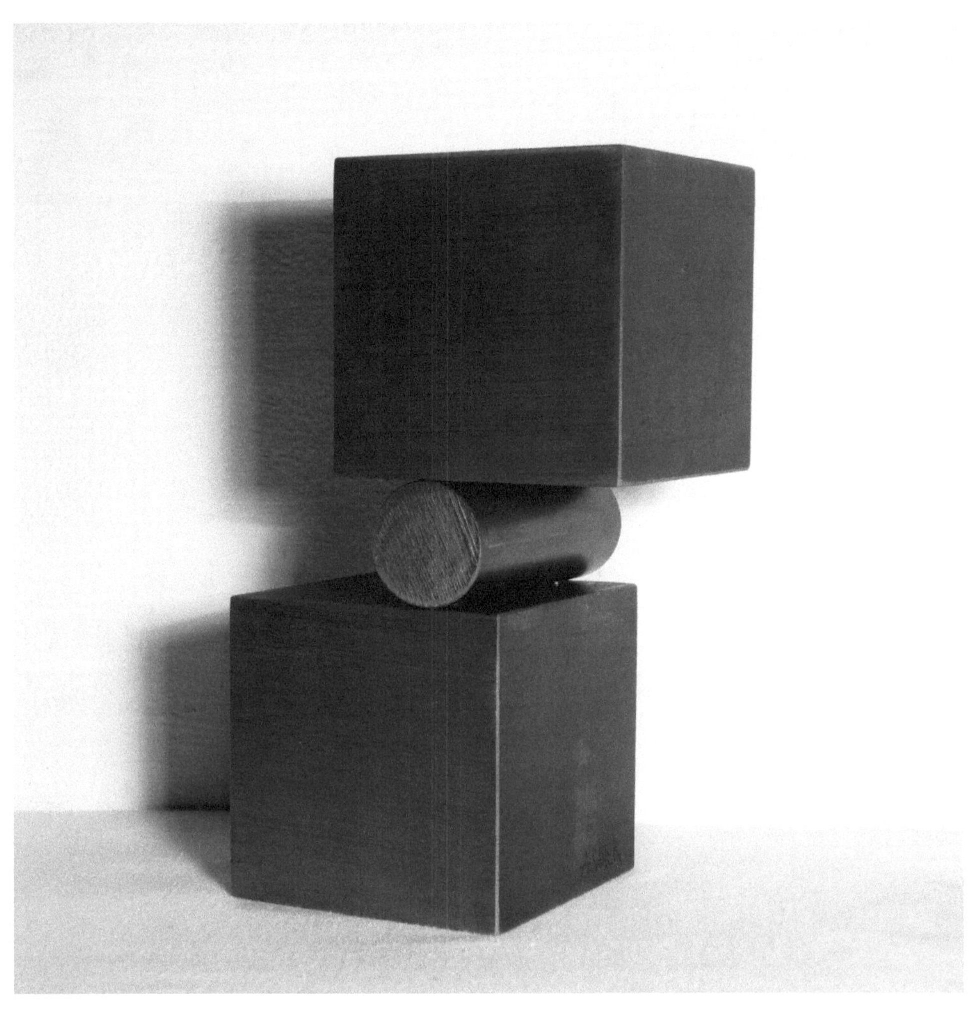

Balance, 10x15x24 cm, steel

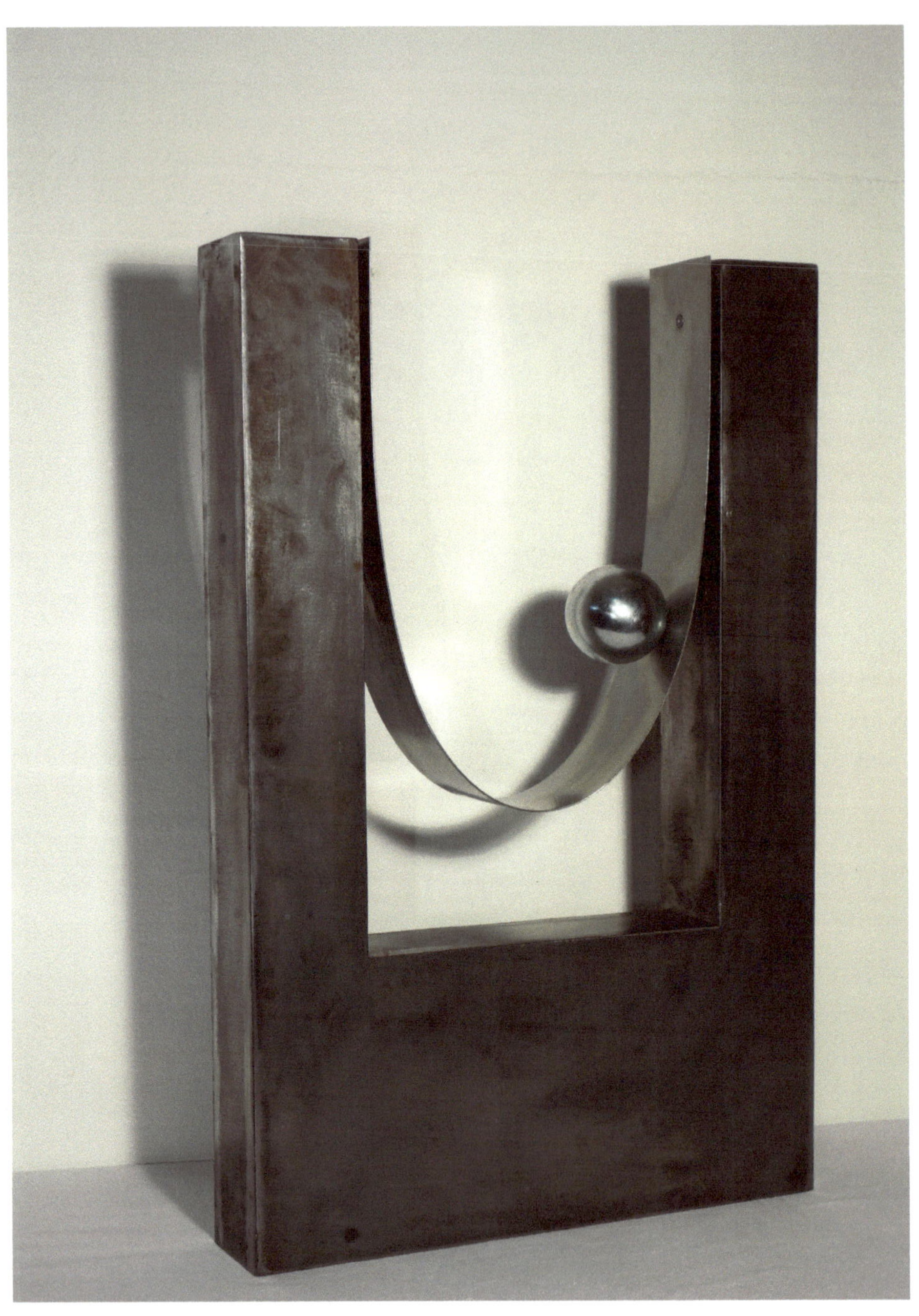

Dynamic - Static 33, 9x48x75 cm, steel

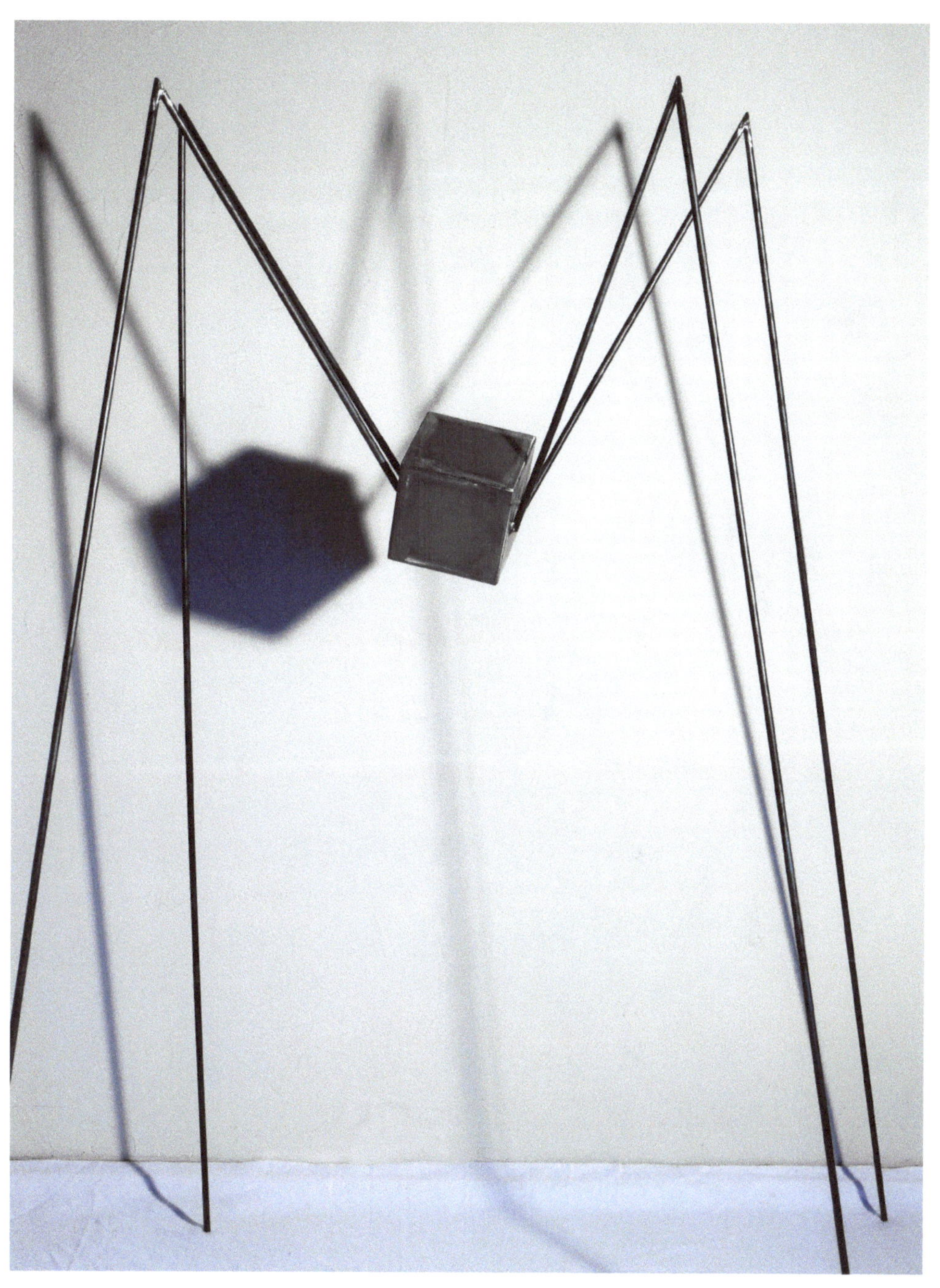

Virus, 100x140x200 cm, steel

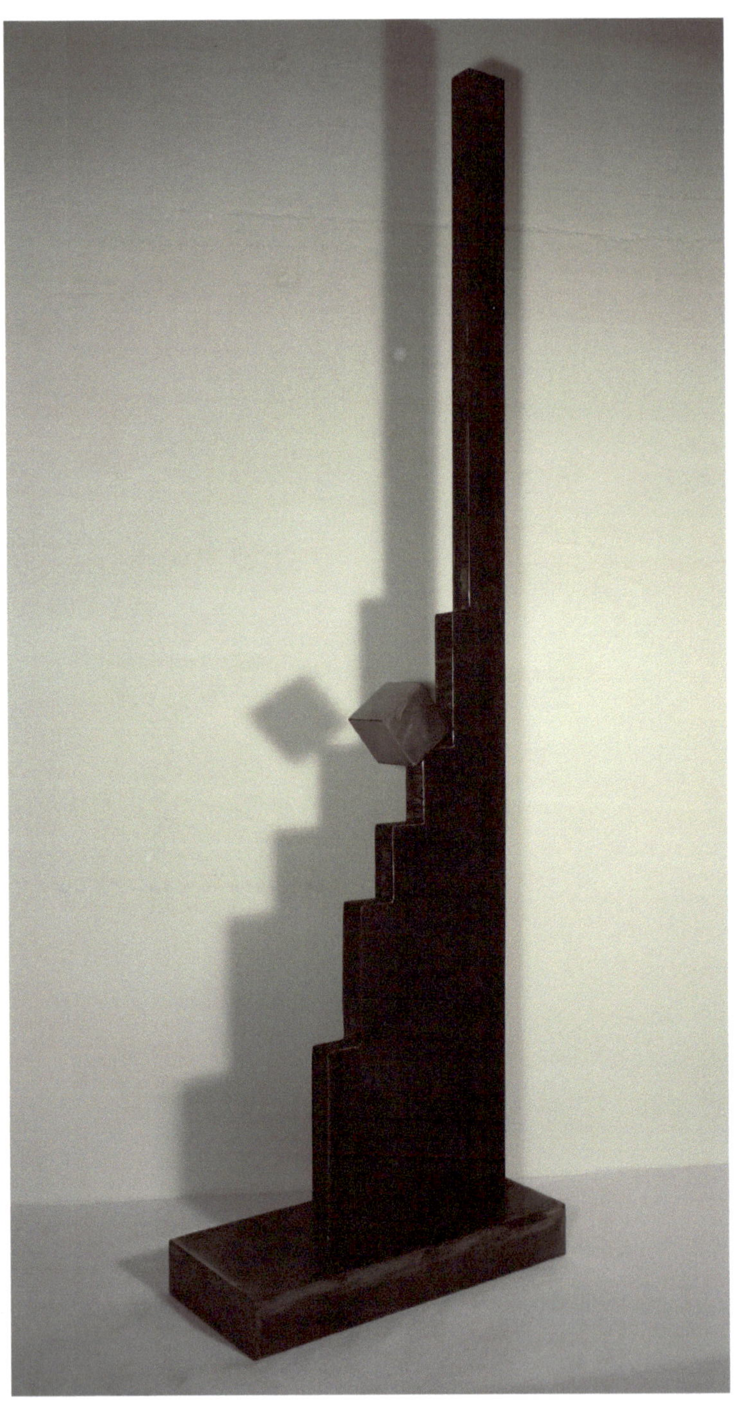

Dynamic - Static 44, 22x48x161 cm, steel

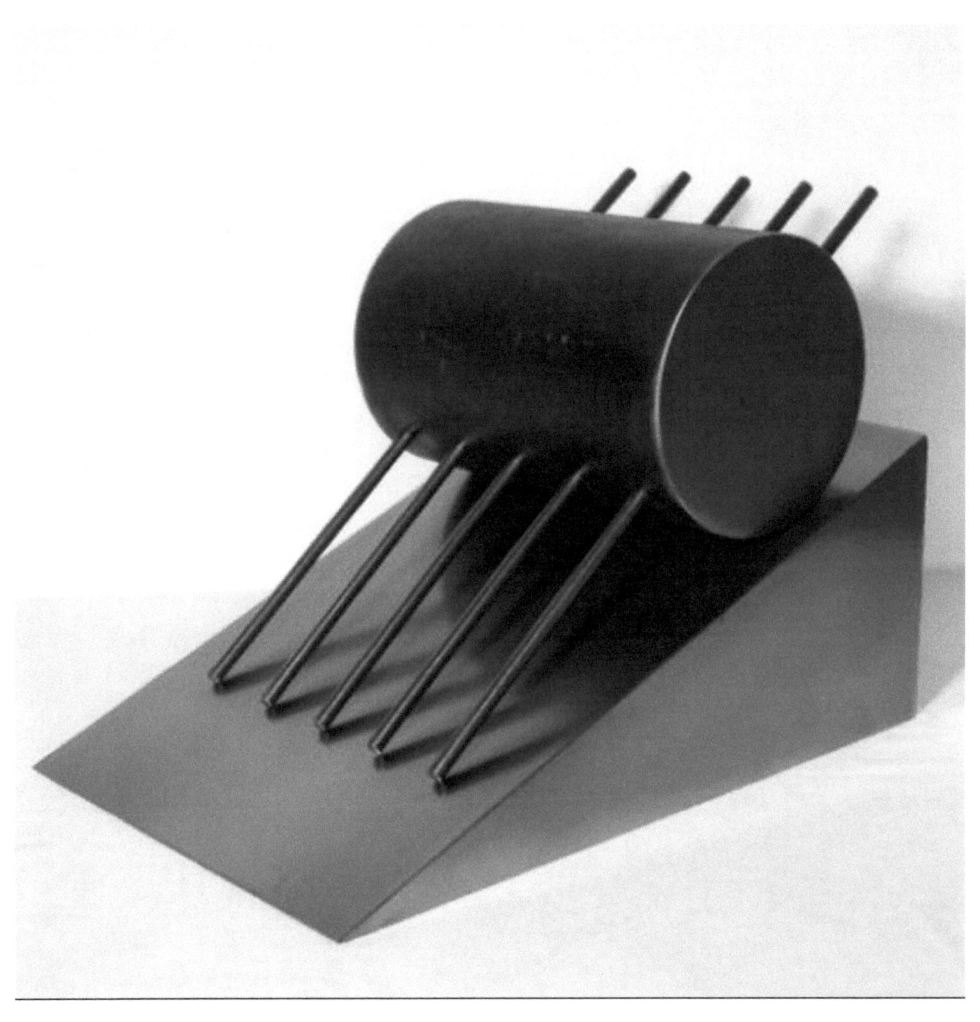

Static 5, 35x51x57 cm, steel

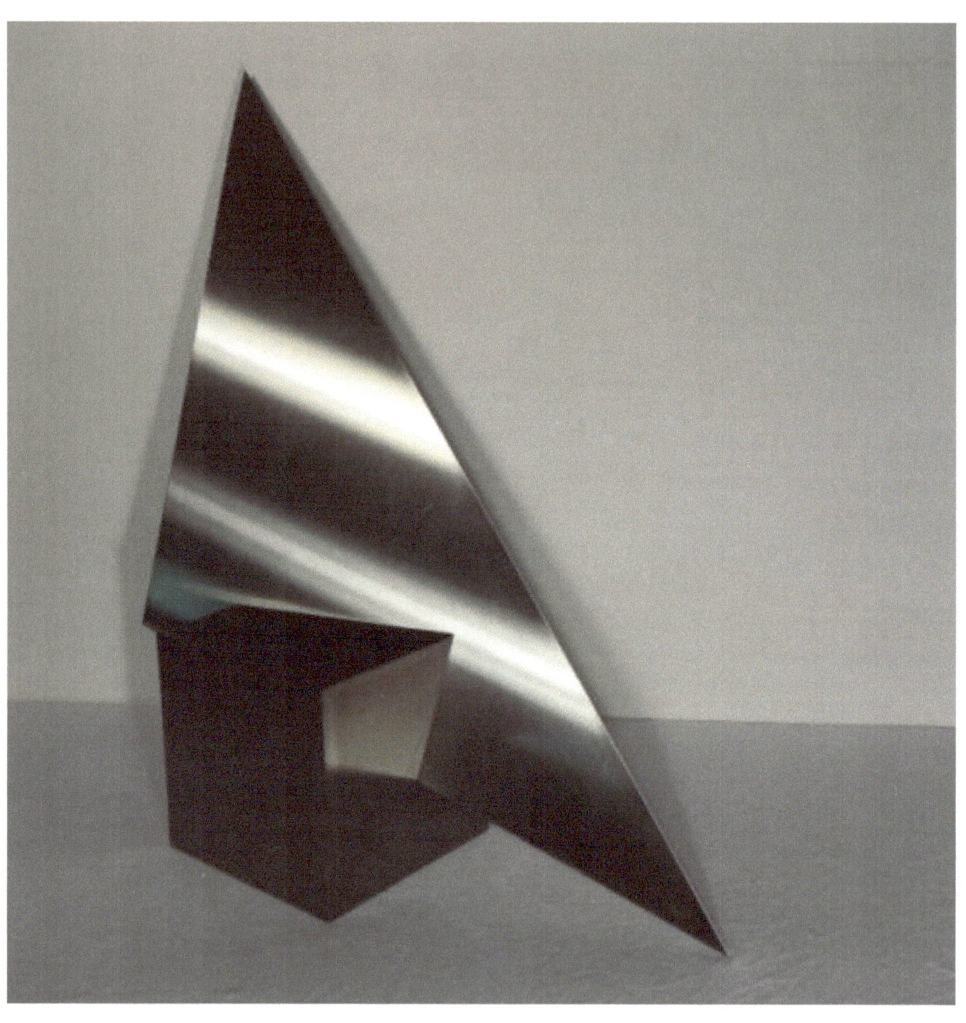

Cut 77, 90x80x26 cm, steel

Swiss artist, autodidact, lives in CH-4226 Breitenbach, nearby Basel. In early years active as Cartoonist for newspapers, entertainment and advertising. Since 1993 three dimensional art: sculptures, objects, photography.
"IRONic animals": Ironic iron animals. Iron-steel sculptures.
"No-thing-objects": We don't know what we are producing. We produce No-things. Wall objects.
"dynamic-statics": The observer as the dynamic part of a static sculpture. The Mental Mobile.
Steel sculptures. Steel sculptures: "Tensions", "Statics" and others in any sizes.
"Silence": Photography. Silence/nature. The search for the contemplative moment.
"Do-it-yourself-Art": A new concept for art installations in the digital age of globalization. Art is created in the absence of the artist.
Ideas transfer instead of matter transfer. Without identification or signature.
Following statements of creative personalities influence my artistic work:

"Art is the elimination everything superfluous."
"The greatest complexity is the greatest simplicity."
"Clarity through simplicity."
"If nothing can be taken away, the work is completed."

Awards 2015- Sandro Botticelli Prize, Florenz; Roma Imperiale, International Prize, Rome; Marco Polo, International Prize, Venice; Il David di Gian Lorenzo Bernini, International Art Award, Lecce 2015 Michelangelo, International Prize, Rome; MAMAG Modern Art Prize, Austria 2016- Leonardo da Vinci, International Prize, Florence; Canaletto Prize, Artistic Career Award Premio International Prize Tiepolo, Arte Milano International Prize Colosseo, Rome 2017- Artist of the month March 2017, artavita, USA.

Exhibitions: Basel, Zürich, Lausanne, Ascona, Meisterschwanden, Mannheim, Lörrach, Salzburg, Lausanne, Ortona, La Valletta Malta, Edinburgh, Ontario, Palermo, Rome, Vatican, Verona, Venezia, Monaco, Cannes, Vienna, Ontario, Paris, Miami, Manhattan/New York.

Artista svizzero, autodidatta, vive a Breitenbach, nelle vicinanze di Basilea. Nei primi anni della sua carriera è stato attivo come vignettista per i giornali il divertimento e la pubblicità. Dal 1993 arte tridimensionale: scultura, oggetti, fotografia.
"IRONic animals": animali ironici di ferro (iron) sculture di ferro-acciaio
"No-thing-objects": Non sappiamo cosa stiamo producendo. Produciamo No-things (no-cose). Oggetti murali.
Steel sculptures (sculture in acciaio): "Tensions", "Statics" e altre in tutte le dimensioni.
"Silence": fotografia. Silenzio/natura. La ricerca del momento contemplativo.
"Do-it-yourself-Art": (arte fai da te) un nuovo concetto per istallazioni artistiche nell'epoca della globalizzazione digitale. L'arte è creata in assenza dell'artista. Trasferimento di idee invece di trasferimento materico. Senza identificazione o firma. Le seguenti frasi di personalità creative influenzano il mio lavoro d'artista:

"Arte è l'eliminare ogni superfluo."
"La grandissima complessità è la grandissima semplicità."
"Chiarezza per mezzo della semplicità."
"Se nulla può essere portato via, l'opera è completa."

Premi: 2015- Premio Sandro Botticelli, Firenze; Premio Internazionale "Roma imperiale", Roma; premio internazionale "Marco Polo", Venezia; Il David di Gian Lorenzo Bernini, Premio d'arte internazionale, Lecce; Premio Internazionale "Michelangelo", Roma; "MAMAG" premio d'arte moderna, Austria 2016: Premio internazionale "Leonardo Da Vinci", Firenze; premio artistico alla carriera "Canaletto"; premio internazionale "Tiepolo" Arte Milano, premio internazionale "Colosseo", Roma 2017: Artista del mese (marzo 2017), Artavita, USA.

Mostre: Basilea, Zurigo, Losanna, Ascona, Meisterschwanden, Mannheim, Lörrach, Salisburgo, Losanna, Ortona, La Valletta Malta, Edimburgo, Ontario, Palermo, Roma, Vaticano, Verona, Venezia, Monaco, Cannes, Vienna, Ontario, Parigi, Miami, Manhattan/New York.

"Alexander Saner - My artistic diary" is an editorial product of Studio Byblos. Every reproduction even partial of the name, of the layout and of the ways of the publication if not authorized by Studio Byblos, will be punished by according the law. The typographic printing and the reprint of the publication is an exclusive of Studio Byblos, which allows the diffusion of a single page or of all the publication in image format. The publication in digital platforms must occur exclusively after authorization of Studio Byblos. The author right on the artworks are of Mr. Alexander Saner. The addresses of Mr. Alexander Saner and the images have been published according his consent. The comment by Dino Marasà cannot be reproduced, cannot be translated or be modified, without his approval. For any dispute the Court of Palermo will be exclusively competent.

"Alexander Saner - Il mio diario d'artista" è un prodotto editoriale di Studio Byblos. Qualsiasi riproduzione anche parziale del nome, del progetto grafico, delle modalità di pubblicazione non autorizzata da Studio Byblos sarà perseguita secondo i termini di legge. La stampa della pubblicazione e delle ristampe è esclusiva di Studio Byblos, il quale consente la diffusione di singole pagine o del libro intero in formato immagine. La pubblicazione su piattaforme digitali deve avvenire esclusivamente con il consenso di Studio Byblos. I diritti sulle opere d'arte sono di proprietà esclusiva del Signor Alexander Saner che ha dato il suo consenso per la pubblicazione delle stesse e dei loro recapiti. La presentazione di Dino Marasà non può essere riprodotta, modificata, tradotta senza consenso dello stesso. Per qualsiasi controversia si elegge competente il Foro di Palermo.

www.ingramcontent.com/pod-product-compliance
Lightning Source LLC
LaVergne TN
LVHW051458180726
843512LV00001B/87